No one knows for sure how Pooh got his name. But whenever a fly settled on his nose he said "Pooh!" to blow it away – so perhaps that's why he came to be called Winnie the Pooh.

Winnie the Pooh liked to have 'A Little Something' around eleven o'clock every morning. Best of all he liked honey. So one day Pooh went out to find the honey tree… and had a dreadful time with some very angry bees…

British Library Cataloguing in Publication Data
Walt Disney's Winnie the Pooh and the honey tree.
  I. Disney, Walt, *1901-1966*
  813'.54 [J]
  ISBN 0-7214-1196-7

First edition

Published by Ladybird Books Ltd Loughborough Leicestershire UK

Printed in England

DISNEY

WINNIE THE POOH
and the Honey Tree

Ladybird Books

Winnie the Pooh was very fond of honey. He could lick out a honey pot until there was nothing left except a little bit of stickiness round the rim.

Every morning at about eleven o'clock Pooh liked to have A Little Something. And that Little Something was usually honey.

Pooh was so greedy that he could eat a whole pot of honey and still feel hungry.

He ate and ate and his tummy got

fatter and fatter. Then one day he
burst at the seams, and his friend
Christopher Robin had to mend
him with a needle and thread.

Pooh decided it was time to do his
stoutness exercises. As he did them,
he hummed a tune so that the
exercises wouldn't seem such hard
work.

He stretched his short arms up in the air, then bent down to touch his toes. He did try very hard, but he couldn't quite reach them.

Pooh had just sat down to have a rest when he suddenly heard a buzzing sound. And he knew what made that buzzing sound – bees.

Bees meant only one thing to Pooh – honey.

He was sitting under a honey tree!

At once Pooh started to climb the
honey tree. As he climbed, he
hummed a little tune to himself.

He was so busy climbing and
humming that he didn't notice how
thin the branches were.

All of a sudden there was a loud
CRACK! The branch Pooh was
holding snapped, and he slipped.
Then he bounced from branch to
branch, and landed with a crash in
a gorse bush.

Poor old Pooh! He crawled out of
the bush and picked the prickles
out of his fur. He was now a very
cross, hungry little bear.

Then Pooh had an idea. He went
to see his friend Christopher
Robin.

"I wonder," said Pooh, "if you've
such a thing as a balloon about
you?"

"Why do you want a balloon?"
asked Christopher Robin.

Pooh put his paw to his mouth and
said in a deep whisper, "Honey!"

"No one gets honey with balloons!" said Christopher Robin.

"I do," replied Pooh. "When you go after honey, you mustn't let the bees know you're coming. So if I have a blue balloon, they may think I'm only part of the sky."

He thought for a moment, then he added, "I shall try to look like a small black cloud. That will trick them." And he rolled about in a muddy puddle until he was black all over.

Christopher Robin thought Pooh was being rather silly, but since he did have a blue balloon, he gave it to Pooh.

Pooh took the balloon, and almost at once a gust of wind lifted him up into the air.

He floated up towards the honey
tree, then stretched out his paw and
scooped up some delicious honey.

He was feeling very pleased with
himself, until he saw that his paw
was covered with bees. They were
buzzing angrily.

"Oh dear!" cried Pooh. "I think the bees suspect something!" Then he shouted to Christopher Robin who was down below, "I say, Christopher Robin, you could help me to trick the bees! Put up

your umbrella and say, 'Oh my, it looks like rain!'"

Christopher Robin put up his umbrella. "Oh my, it looks like rain!" he said.

But the bees continued to buzz
angrily around Pooh.

Then the string holding Pooh's
balloon came undone and the air
inside escaped with a rush.

Pooh went zooming through the sky
at great speed, then landed safely in
Christopher Robin's arms.

But the bees went on buzzing, "Thief!
Thief! You tried to steal our honey!"

Then Christopher Robin had an idea. He and Pooh jumped into the muddy puddle and hid under the umbrella. The bees would not find them there.

Pooh was pleased to be sitting in a muddy puddle. It was one of his most favourite places to play.

The bees buzzed around angrily for a while, looking for Pooh and Christopher Robin, but they couldn't see them. The umbrella made a good hiding place.

At last the bees returned to their
tree, and Christopher Robin and
Pooh crept out from their hiding
place. They looked just like *two*
little black rainclouds now!

By the time they were clean again,
Pooh decided he could do with
A Little Something.

He picked up one of his honey
pots, and ate and ate until his
tummy was full.

He was a very happy, very sticky
little bear. He had had a terrible
adventure with the bees, but the
day had ended splendidly after all.

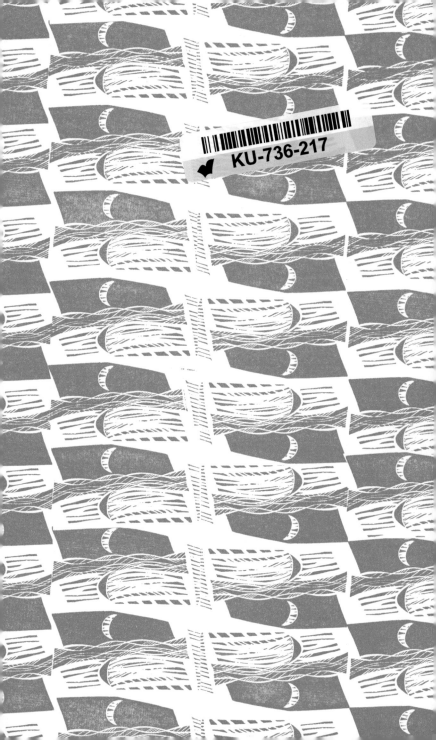

DART

Dart

ALICE OSWALD

faber and faber

First published in 2002
by Faber and Faber Ltd
Bloomsbury House
74–77 Great Russell Street
London WC1B 3DA
This special Poetry Firsts edition first published in 2010
Typeset by Wilmaset Limited, Wirral
Printed and bound in the UK by CPI Mackays, Chatham

A CIP record for this book
is available from the British Library

ISBN 978-0-571-25933-5

2 4 6 8 10 9 7 5 3 1

DART

Acknowledgements

Too many people have helped with this poem for me to mention them all, but the following, in no particular order, have made significant contributions:

Tom Greeves
Iain Mounsy
Steven Westcott
Sue Bragg
Anonymous walker
Peter Oswald
Judy Gordan-Jones
Mark Beeson
David Pakes
Mike Maslin
Rupert Lane
Susan Clifford
Angela King
Steve Roberts
John Wilson
Andrew Dutfield
Eddie Campbell Thomas
Nigel Gibson
Mike Ingram (for National Trust)
Charles and Mary Keen
William Keen
Ellie Keen
Laura Beatty
Barrie Lorring
3 anonymous poachers
Joe and Lyle Oswald
Bram Bartlett

Gerry
Ric and Angie Palmer
Simon Ellyatt
Chris Scoble
Richard Scoble
Jim Scoble
Ted Bloomfield
Kevin Pyne
Sid Griffiths
Matt Griffiths
John Riddel
Jilly Sutton
Jane Hill
Sean Borodale
Caroline Drew
Captain Dadd
Kirsten Saunders
John Lane
The Trustees of Dartington Hall
Chris Burcher
Trudy Turrell
Tim Robins
Ray Humphries
Tony Dixon
Roger Deakin
Colin Hawkins

This poem was written and developed as part of the Poetry Society's Poetry Places scheme funded by the 'Arts for Everyone' budget of the Arts Council of England's Lottery Department.

This poem is made from the language of people who live and work on the Dart. Over the past two years I've been recording conversations with people who know the river. I've used these records as life-models from which to sketch out a series of characters – linking their voices into a sound-map of the river, a songline from the source to the sea. There are indications in the margin where one voice changes into another. These do not refer to real people or even fixed fictions. All voices should be read as the river's mutterings.

A.O.

Who's this moving alive over the moor?

An old man seeking and finding a difficulty.

Has he remembered his compass his spare socks
does he fully intend going in over his knees off the
    military track from Okehampton?

keeping his course through the swamp spaces
and pulling the distance around his shoulders

the source of the Dart
– Cranmere Pool on
Dartmoor, seven
miles from the nearest
road

and if it rains, if it thunders suddenly
where will he shelter looking round
and all that lies to hand is his own bones?

tussocks, minute flies,
      wind, wings, roots

He consults his map. A huge rain-coloured wilderness.
This must be the stones, the sudden movement,
the sound of frogs singing in the new year.
Who's this issuing from the earth?

The Dart, lying low in darkness calls out Who is it?
trying to summon itself by speaking ...

the walker replies

An old man, fifty years a mountaineer, until my heart gave out,
so now I've taken to the moors. I've done all the walks, the Two
Moors Way, the Tors, this long winding line the Dart

this secret buried in reeds at the beginning of sound I
won't let go of man, under
his soakaway ears and his eye ledges working
into the drift of his thinking, wanting his heart

I keep you folded in my mack pocket and I've marked in red
where the peat passes are and the good sheep tracks

1

cow-bones, tin-stones, turf-cuts.
listen to the horrible keep-time of a man walking,
rustling and jingling his keys
at the centre of his own noise,
clomping the silence in pieces and I

I don't know, all I know is walking. Get dropped off the military track from Oakehampton and head down into Cranmere pool. It's dawn, it's a huge sphagnum kind of wilderness, and an hour in the morning is worth three in the evening. You can hear plovers whistling, your feet sink right in, it's like walking on the bottom of a lake.

What I love is one foot in front of another. South-south-west and down the contours. I go slipping between Black Ridge and White Horse Hill into a bowl of the moor where echoes can't get out

listen,
a
lark
spinning
around
one
note
splitting
and
mending
it

and I find you in the reeds, a trickle coming out of a bank, a foal of a river

one step-width water
of linked stones
trills in the stones
glides in the trills
eels in the glides
in each eel a fingerwidth of sea

in walking boots, with twenty pounds on my back: spare socks,
compass, map, water purifier so I can drink from streams, seeing
the cold floating spread out above the morning,

tent, torch, chocolate, not much else.

Which'll make it longish, almost unbearable between my
evening meal and sleeping, when I've got as far as stopping,
sitting in the tent door with no book, no saucepan, not so much
as a stick to support the loneliness

he sits clasping his knees, holding his face low down
    between them,
he watches black slugs,
he makes a little den of his smells and small thoughts
he thinks up a figure far away on the tors
waving, so if something does happen,
if night comes down and he has to leave the path
then we've seen each other, somebody knows where
    we are.

falling back on appropriate words

turning the loneliness in all directions ...

through Broadmarsh,   under Cut Hill,

Sandyhole, Sittaford, Hartyland, Postbridge,

Belever, Newtake, Dartmeet, the whole
unfolding emptiness branching and reaching
and bending over itself.

I met a man sevenish by the river
where it widens under the main road
and adds a strand strong enough
to break branches and bend back necks.

Rain. Not much of a morning.
Routine work, getting the buckets out

and walking up the cows – I know you,
Jan Coo. A wind on a deep pool.

Cows know him, looking for the fork in the dark.
They know the truth of him – a strange man –
I'm soaked, fuck these numb hands.
A tremor in the woods. A salmon under a stone.

I know who I am, I
come from the little heap of stones up by Postbridge,
you'll have seen me feeding the stock, you can tell it's
    me
because of the wearing action of water on bone.

Oh I'm slow and sick, I'm
trying to talk myself round to leaving this place,
but there's roots growing round my mouth, my foot's
in a rusted tin. One night I will.

And so one night he sneaks away downriver,
told us he could hear voices woooo
we know what voices means, Jan Coo Jan Coo.
A white feather on the water keeping dry.

Next morning it came home to us he was drowned.
He should never have swum on his own.
Now he's so thin you can see the light
through his skin, you can see the filth in his midriff.

Now he's the groom of the Dart – I've seen him
taking the shape of the sky, a bird, a blade,
a fallen leaf, a stone – may he lie long
in the inexplicable knot of the river's body

in a place of bracken and scattered stone piles and cream teas in
the tourist season, comes the chambermaid unlocking every
morning with her peach-soap hands: Only me, Room-Cleaning,
number twenty-seven, an old couple – he's blind, she's in her
nineties. They come every month walking very slowly to the

Jan Coo: his name
means So-and-So of
the Woods, he haunts
the Dart

Postbridge is where
the first road crosses
the Dart

chambermaid

4

waterfall. She guides him, he props her. She sees it, he hears it.
Gently resenting each other's slowness: (Where are we turning
you are tending to slide is it mud what is that long word
meaning burthensome it's as if mud was issuing from ourselves
don't step on the trefoil listen a lark going up in the dark would
you sshhhhh?) Brush them away, squirt everything, bleach and
vac and rubberglove them into a bin-bag, please do not leave
toenails under the rugs, a single grey strand in the basin

shhh I can make myself invisible   Naturalist
with binoculars in moist places. I can see frogs
hiding under spawn – water's sperm – whisper, I wear
    soft colours

whisper, this is the naturalist
she's been out since dawn
dripping in her waterproof notebook

I'm hiding in red-brown grass all different lengths, bog bean,
sundew, I get excited by its wetness, I watch spiders watching
aphids, I keep my eyes in crevices, I know two secret places, call
them x and y where the Large Blue Butterflies are breeding, it's
lovely, the male chasing the female, frogs singing lovesongs

she loves songs, she belongs to the soundmarks of larks

I knew a heron once, when it got up
its wings were the width of the river,
I saw it eat an eel alive
and the eel the eel chewed its way back inside out
    through the heron's stomach
like when I creep through bridges right in along a ledge
    to see where the dippers nest.
Going through holes, I love that, the last thing through
    here was an otter

(two places I've seen eels, bright whips of flow   by the bridge, an eel
like stopper waves the rivercurve slides through   watcher
trampling around at first you just make out

the elver movement of the running sunlight
three foot under the road-judder you hold
and breathe contracted to an eye-quiet world
while an old dandelion unpicks her shawl
and one by one the small spent oak flowers fall
then gently lift a branch brown tag and fur
on every stone and straw and drifting burr
when like a streamer from your own eye's iris
a kingfisher spurts through the bridge whose axis
is endlessly in motion as each wave
photos its flowing to the bridge's curve
if you can keep your foothold, snooping down
then suddenly two eels let go get thrown
tumbling away downstream looping and linking
another time we scooped a net through sinking
silt and gold and caught one strong as bike-chain
stared for a while then let it back again
I never pass that place and not make time
to see if there's an eel come up the stream
I let time go as slow as moss, I stand
and try to get the dragonflies to land
their gypsy-coloured engines on my hand)

whose voice is this who's talking in my larynx
who's in my privacy under my stone tent
where I live slippershod in my indoor colours
who's talking in my lights-out where I pull to
under the bent body of an echo are these your
fingers in my roof are these your splashes

Everyone converges on bridges, bank holidays it fills up with
cars, people set up tables in the reeds, but a mile either side
you're back into wilderness. (*Twelve horses clattering away.*) and
there's the dipper bobbing up and down like a man getting
ready, hitching his trousers. I'm crouching, I never let my
reflection fall on water,

I depend on being not noticed, which keeps me small and rather nimble, I can swim miles naked with midges round my head, watching wagtails, I'm soft, I'm an otter streaking from the headwaters, I run overland at night, I watch badgers, I trespass, don't say anything, I've seen waternymphs, I've seen tiny creatures flying, trapped, intermarrying, invisible

upriver creatures born into this struggle against
water out of balance being swept away
mouthparts clinging to mosses

round streamlined creatures born into vanishing
between golden hide-outs, trout at the mercy of rush
quiver to keep still always

swimming up through it hiding
freshwater shrimps driven flat in this struggle against
haste pitching through stones

things suck themselves to rocks
things swinging from side to side
leak out a safety line to a leaf and

grip for dear life a sandgrain or gravel for ballast
thrown into this agony of being swept away
with ringing everywhere though everything is also silent

the spider of the rapids running over the repeated note
of disorder and rhythm in collision, the simulacrum fly
spinning a shelter of silk among the stones

and all the bright-feathered flies of the fishermen, indignant under the waterfall, in waders, getting their feet into position to lean over and move the world: medics, milkmen, policemen, millionaires, cheering themselves up with the ratchet and swish of their lines

fisherman and bailiff

I've payed fifty pounds to fish here and I fish like hell, I know the etiquette – who wades where – and I know the dark places under stones where things are moving. I caught one thirteen pounds at

7

Belever, huge, silvery, maybe seven times back from the sea, now the sea-trout, he's canny, he'll keep to his lie till you've gone, you have to catch him at night.

Which is where the law comes in, the bailiff, as others see me, as I see myself when I wake, finding myself in this six-foot fourteen-stone of flesh with letters after my name, in boots, in a company vehicle, patrolling from the headwaters to the weir, with all my qualified faculties on these fish.

When the owls are out up at Newtake. You cast behind and then forwards in two actions. Casting into darkness for this huge, it's like the sea's right there underneath you, this invisible

now I know my way round darkness, I've got night vision, I've been up here in the small hours waiting for someone to cosh me but

it's not frightening if you know what you're doing. There's a sandbar, you can walk on it right across the weirpool but

I hooked an arm once, petrified, slowly pulling a body up, it was only a cardigan

but when you're onto a salmon,
a big one hiding under a rock, you can see his tail
    making the water move,
you let the current work your fly

all the way from Iceland, from the Faroes,
a three-sea-winter fish coming up on the spate,
on the full moon, when the river spreads out

a thousand feet between Holne and Dartmeet and he
    climbs it,
up the trickiest line, maybe
maybe down-flowing water has an upcurrent nobody
    knows

it takes your breath away,
generations of them inscribed into this river,
up at Belever where the water's only so wide

you can see them crowded in there
shining like tin, the hen-fish swishing her tail
making a little vortex, lifting the gravel

which is where the law comes in – I know all the articles, I hide
in the bushes with my diploma and along comes the Tavistock
boys, they've only got to wet their arms and grab, it's like
shoplifting. Names I won't mention. In broad daylight, in the
holding pools. Run up and stone the water and the salmon
dodges under a ledge. Copper snares, three-pronged forks – I
know what goes on, I'm upfront but I'm tactful.

I wear green for the sake of kingfishers.

I walk across the weir, on the phone in the middle of
   the river,
technically effective, at ease in my own power,
working my way downstream doing rod-license checks

with his torch, taking his own little circle of light
through pole-straight pinewoods,
slippy oakwoods, sudden insurrections of rowan,
reedholes and poor sour fields,
in the thick of bracken, keeping the law
from dwindling away

through Belever Whiteslade

Babeny

Newtake

(meanwhile the West Dart pours through
Crow Tor Fox Holes
Longaford Beardown and Wystman's Wood
and under Crockern Tor, singing

the West Dart rises
under Cut Hill, not
far from the source of
the East Dart

where's Ernie? Under the ground

where's Redver's Webb? Likewise.

Tom, John and Solomon Warne, Dick Jorey, Lewis
    Evely?

Some are photos, others dust.
Heading East to West along the tin lodes,
80 foot under Hexworthy, each with a tallow candle in
    his hat.

Till rain gets into the stone,
which washes them down to the valley bottoms
and iron, lead, zinc, copper calcite
and gold, a few flakes of it
getting pounded between the pebbles in the river.

Bert White, John Coaker.
Frank Hellier, Frank Rensfield,
William Withycombe, Alex Shawe, John Dawe, William
    Friend,
their strength dismantled and holding only names

Two Bridges, Dunnabridge, Hexworthy)

Dartmeet – a mob of waters
where East Dart smashes into West Dart

two wills gnarling and recoiling
and finally knuckling into balance

in that brawl of mudwaves
the East Dart speaks Whiteslade and Babeny

the West Dart speaks a wonderful dark fall
from Cut Hill through Wystman's Wood

put your ear to it, you can hear water
cooped up in moss and moving

slowly uphill through lean-to trees
where every day the sun gets twisted and shut

with the weak sound of the wind
rubbing one indolent twig upon another

and the West Dart speaks roots in a pinch of clitters
the East Dart speaks coppice and standards

the East Dart speaks the Gawler Brook and the
    Wallabrook
the West dart speaks the Blackabrook that runs by the
    prison

at loggerheads, lying next to one another on the
    riverbed
wrangling away into this valley of oaks

forester

and here I am coop-felling in the valley, felling small sections to give the forest some structure. When the chainsaw cuts out the place starts up again. It's Spring, you can work in a wood and feel the earth turning

woodman working on your own   waternymph
knocking the long shadows down
and all day the river's eyes
peep and pry among the trees

when the lithe water turns   Dart is old Devonian
and its tongue flatters the ferns   for oak
do you speak this kind of sound:
whirlpool whisking round?

Listen, I can clap and slide
my hollow hands along my side.
imagine the bare feel of water,
woodman, to the wrinkled timber

When nesting starts I move out. Leaving the thickety places for the birds. Redstart, Pied Flycatchers. Or if I'm thinning, say

every twelve trees I'll orange-tape what I want to keep. I'll find a
fine one, a maiden oak, well-formed with a good crop of acorns
and knock down the trees around it. And that tree'll stand
getting slowly thicker and taller, taking care of its surroundings,
full of birds and moss and cavities where bats'll roost and fly out
when you work into dusk

woodman working into twilight
you should see me in the moonlight
comb my cataract of hair,
at work all night on my desire

oh I could sing a song of Hylas,
how the water wooed him senseless,
I could sing the welded kiss
continuous of Salmacis

and bring an otter from your bowels
to slip in secret through my veils
to all the plump and bony pools
the dips the paps the folds the holes

Trees like that, when they fall the whole place feels different,
different air, different creatures entering the gap. I saw two roe
deer wandering through this morning. And then the wind's got its
foot in and singles out the weaklings, drawn up old coppice stems
that've got no branches to give them balance. I generally leave the
deadwood lying. They say all rivers were once fallen trees. Or tush
it to one of the paths, stacks of it with bracket fungus and it goes
for pulp or pallets or half-cleave it into fence-stakes

woodman working on the crags
alone among increasing twigs
notice this, next time you pause
to drink a flask and file the saws

the Combestone and the Broadstone
standing in a sunbeam gown,

the O Brook and the Rowbrook
starlit everywhere you look

such deep woods it feels like indoors and then you look down
and see it's raining on the river

O Rex Nemorensis

the King of the
Oakwoods who had
to be sacrificed to a
goddess.

Oaks whose arms
are whole trees

in spring when

'Dart Dart
Every year thou
Claimest a heart.'

the river gives
up her dead

I saw you
rise dragging your
shadows in water

all summer I
saw you soaked
through and sinking

and the crack
and shriek as
you lost bones

God how I
wish I could
bury death deep

under the river
like that canoeist

near Newbridge, a
canoeist drowned

just testing his

strokes in the
quick moving water
which buried him

O Flumen Dialis

River of Zeus, the god
of the Oak. In ancient
times the Flamen
Dialis was the priest
of Zeus

let him be
the magical flame

13

come spring that
lights one oak
off the next

and the fields
and workers bursting
into light amen

canoeist

On Tuesdays we come out of the river at twilight, wet, shouting, with canoes on our heads.

the river at ease, the river at night.

We can't hear except the booming of our thinking in the cockpit hollow and the river's been so beautiful we can't concentrate.

they walk strong in wetsuits,
their faces shine,
their well-being wants to burst out

In the water it's another matter, we're just shells and arms, keeping ourselves in a fluid relation with the danger.

pond-skaters, water-beetles,
neoprene spray-decks,
many-coloured helmets,

But what I love is midweek between Dartmeet and Newbridge; kayaking down some inaccessible section between rocks and oaks in a valley gorge which walkers can't get at. You're utterly alone, abandoning everything at every instant, yourself in continuous transition twisting down a steep gradient: big bony boulders, water squeezing in between them. sumps and boils and stopper waves. Times when the river goes over a rock, it speeds up, it slaps into the slower water ahead of it and backs up on itself, literally curls over and you get white water sometimes as high as a bus or house. Like last November, the river rose three or four foot in two hours, right into the fields and I drove like mad to get to Newbridge. I could hear this roaring like some horrible revolving cylinder, I was getting into the river, I hadn't

warmed up, it was still raining, and the surface looked mad,
touchy, ready to slide over, and there was this fence underwater,
a wave whacked me into it

come falleth in my push-you where it hurts
and let me rough you under, be a laugh
and breathe me please in whole inhale

come warmeth, I can outcanoevre you
into the smallest small where it moils up
and masses under the sloosh gates, put your head,

it looks a good one, full of kiss
and known to those you love, come roll it on my stones,
come tongue-in-skull, come drinketh, come sleepeth

I was pinioned by the pressure, the whole river-power of
Dartmoor, not even five men pulling on a rope could shift
me. It was one of those experiences – I was sideways, leaning
upstream, a tattered shape in a perilous relationship with time

will you rustle quietly and listen to what I have to say
    now
describing the wetbacks of stones golden-mouthed and
making no headway, will you unsilt

how water orders itself like a pack of geese goes up
first in tatters then in shreds then in threads
and shucking its pools crawls into this slate and thin
    limestone phase

three hayfields above Buckfast where annual meadow
    grasshoppers
flower and fly to the tune of ribbed stalks rubbed.
will you swim down and attend to this foundry for
    sounds

this jabber of pidgin-river
drilling these rhythmic cells and trails of scales,
will you translate for me blunt blink glint.

is it span of eyes trammelling under the rain-making
    oaks
among stones the colour of magpies is it
suddenly through a padlocked gate

a green lane sliptoes secretly to the unseen
steep woods and cows the far side and
town boys sneak here after school: 'once   town boys

I jumped off the bus, I walked straight across, it was
    ice,
now this is the real river, this is the Queen of the Dart
where it jinks down like through lawns almost'

the way I talk in my many-headed turbulence
among these modulations, this nimbus of words kept in
    motion
sing-calling something definitely human,

will somebody sing this riffle perfectly as the invisible
    river
sings it, quite different from this harsh primary
repertoire of murmurs, without any hardware

of stones and jointed sticks, one note
that rives apart the two worlds without any crossing
'I could show you a place it shallows over rocks

where the salmon flip out sometimes right onto the
    stones or they used to
and you could catch them bare-handed, now listen to
    this,
I was lugging this fish the size of myself,

taking the short-cut through the Abbey and up
picture it, up comes a monk and imagine
he gives me a suitcase to smuggle it out past the
    bailiff ...'

Smuggle it under the threshold of listening
into the ark of the soul, where the invisible
clear first water, the real Dart

writhes like a black fire, smelling of fish and soil
and traces a red leaf flood mark
and catches a drift of placer gold in her cracks

tin-extractor

you can go down with a wide bowl, where it eddies round bends
or large boulders. A special not easy motion, you fill it with
gravel and a fair amount of water, you shake it and settle it and
tilt it forward. You get a bit of gold, enough over the years to
make a wedding ring but mostly these dense black stones what
are they?

He puts them in Hydrochloric acid, it makes his fingers yellow,
but they came up shiny, little wobbly nuts of tin

when I realised what I was onto in my own fields, I began to
work slowly upriver looking for the shodes, the bigger tin-stones
that lie close to the source. I followed it up a brook of the Dart
and built my own alluvial plant with a pump re-circulating the
water and a bucket on a drag-line bopping it out and bingo

Glico of the Running Streams

named varieties of
water

and Spio of the Boulders-Encaved-In-The-River's-
    Edges

and all other named varieties of Water
such as Loops and Swirls in their specific dialects
clucking and clapping

Cymene and Semaia, sweeping a plectrum along the
    stones
and the stones' hollows hooting back at them
off-beat, as if luck should play the flute

can you hear them at all,
                muted and plucked,
muttering something that can only be expressed as

hitting a series of small bells just under the level of your
   listening?

you rinse it through a shaking screen, you take out a ton of
gravelly mud for say fifty pounds of tin and then you smelt it,
1,300 degrees C, that's amazingly hot, that's when steel begins to
burn and just as it turns it starts melting, evaporating, half your
tin disappearing into the air

can you hear them rustling close by,
passing from hand to hand
a little trail of tin more than the weight of stone
and making the swish of swinging and regaining
   equilibrium?

Syrinx and Ligea groping through low-lit stalls
with silt in their mouths,
can you not hear them at all? not even the Rain
starting in several places at once
or a Fly's Foot typing on water?

not even the Stockdove-Falling-
Upwards-Through-Inverted-Trees

and calling prrrrooo prrrooo, who's
stirring the water about, who's up
the green end of the river dislodging stones?

I, Pol de Zinc, descended from the Norman, keeper of the coin,
entrepreneur, allrounder and tin extractor the last of a long line

William Withycombe, Alex Shawe, John Dawe,
   William Friend

and I. Keeper of the Woollen Mills, a fully vertical   worker at Buckfast
   operation,   Woollen Mills
adding a certain amount of detergent, non-ionic,
   reasonably biodegradable,

18

which you have to, when you see how the wool comes in,
greasy with blue paint, shitty and sweaty with droppings
    dangling off it.

Unfortunately sheep don't use loopaper.

it's all very well the fishermen complaining
but I see us like cormorants, living off the river.
we depend on it for its soft water
because it runs over granite and it's relatively free of
    calcium
whereas fishermen for what for leisure

the Woollen Mill has a
license to extract river
water for washing the
wool and for making
up the dyes

tufting felting hanks tops spindles slubbings
hoppers and rollers and slatted belts
bales of carded wool the colour of limestone
and wool puffs flying through tubes distributed by
    cyclones

wool in the back of the throat, wool on ledges,
in fields and spinning at 5,000 rotations per minute –
and look how quickly a worker can mend an end
what tentacular fingers moving like a spider,
splicing it invisibly neat look what fingers could be –

cotton warp, jute weft, wool pile, they work
lip-reading in a knocking throbbing bobbining hubbub
transporting the web on slatted belts with a twist to get it
    transverse,
then out for lunchbreak, hearing the small sounds of the
    day

That smell of old wet sheep.
I can stand by the fleece pile and pick out the different
    breeds:
this coarse lustrous curly one from Dartmoor,
this straighter one's a blackface from Scotland.

19

We pull apart the fleeces and blend them, we get a mountain, a tor of wool, and load it onto hoppers for washing and keep combing it out, because the lie of wool isn't smooth and cylindrical like a human hair, it's scaly like a fish or pine cone, which is why you get felting when the scales get locked and can't release.

We do pure wool, one of the last places – red carpets, for Japenese weddings. Which we dye in pressure vessels, 600 different shades, it's skilled work, a machine with criss-cross motion makes up the hanks and we hang them in the dye-house. Bear in mind if it rains, there's peat in the river-water, full of metals, tin and such-like which when you consider dyes are mostly metals, we split the web and rub it into slubbings and from there onto bobbins we stretch and wind it on a spinning frame – a ring and travel arrangement twists it in the opposite direction and we end up with two-ply, a balanced twist, like the river

Theodore Schwenk

'whenever currents of water meet the confluence is
    always the place
where rhythmical and spiralling movements may arise,
spiralling surfaces which glide past one another in
    manifold winding and curving forms
new water keeps flowing through each single strand of
    water
whole surfaces interweaving spatially and flowing past
    each other
in surface tension, through which water strives to attain
    a spherical drop-form'

wound onto reels and packed into bales
tied with polypropylene and cling film to keep it dry on
    the sea.

all day my voice is being washed away
out of a lapse in my throat

at Staverton Ford,
John Edmunds bei
washed away, 1840

like after rain
little trails of soil-creep
loosen into streams

if I shout out,
if I shout in,
I am only as wide
as a word's aperture

but listen! if you listen
I will move you a few known sounds
in a constant irregular pattern:
flocks of foxgloves spectating slightly bending ...

o I wish I was slammicking home
in wet clothes, shrammed with cold and bivvering but

this is my voice
under the spickety leaves,
under the knee-nappered trees
rustling in its cubby-holes

and rolling me round, like a container
upturned and sounded through

and the silence pouring into what's left maybe eighty
    seconds

Menyahari – we scream in mid-air.
We jump from a tree into a pool, we change ourselves
into the fish dimension. Everybody swims here
under Still Pool Copse, on a saturday,
slapping the water with bare hands, it's fine once you're
    in.

Is it cold? Is it sharp?

I stood looking down through beech trees.
When I threw a stone I could count five before the
    splash.

Then I jumped in a rush of gold to the head,
through black and cold, red and cold, brown and warm,
giving water the weight and size of myself in order to
    imagine it,
water with my bones, water with my mouth and my
    understanding

22

when my body was in some way a wave to swim in,
one continuous fin from head to tail
I steered through rapids like a canoe,
digging my hands in, keeping just ahead of the pace of
    the river,
thinking God I'm going fast enough already, what am I,
spelling the shapes of the letters with legs and arms?

S SSS   W

    Slooshing the Water open and

MMM

    for it Meeting shut behind me

He dives, he shuts himself in a deep soft-bottomed
    silence
which underwater is all nectarine, nacreous. He lifts
the lid and shuts and lifts the lid and shuts and the sky
jumps in and out of the world he loafs in.
Far off and orange in the glow of it he drifts
all down the Deer Park, into the dished and dangerous
    stones of old walls
before the weirs were built, when the sea
came wallowing wide right over these floodfed
    buttercups.

Who's this beside him? Twenty knights at arms
capsized in full metal getting over the creeks;
they sank like coins with the heads on them still
    conscious
between water and steel trying to prize a little niche, a
hesitation, a hiding-place, a breath, helplessly

loosening straps with fingers metalled up, and the river
already counting them into her bag, taking her tythe,   'Dart Dart wants a
who now swim light as decayed spiderweb leaves.   heart'

Poor Kathy Pellam and the scout from Deadman's
     pool
tangled in the river's wires. There they lie
like scratchmarks in a stack of glass,
trapped under panes while he slides by
through Folly Pool through Folly Stickle,
hundreds of people hot from town with snorkels
dinghies minnow jars briefs bikinis
all slowly methodically swimming rid of their jobs.

Now the blessing, the readiness of Christ
be with all those who stare or fall into this river.
May the water buoy them up, may God grant them
extraordinary lifejacket lightness. And this child
watching two salmon glooming through Boathouse Pool
in water as high as heaven, spooked with yew trees
and spokes of wetrot branches – Christ be there
watching him watching, walking on this river.

water abstractor

and may He pull you out at Littlehempston, at the pumphouse,
which is my patch, the world's largest operational Sirofloc plant.
Abstracting water for the whole Torbay area. That and Venford
and the Spine Main

(it's August and a
pendulum gladness swings just
missing our heads by
a millimetre the sun
unwrappers the hedgerows full
of sticky sweets and
sucks and each hour
the river alternates its
minnows through various cubes)

You don't know what goes into water. Tiny particles of acids and salts. Cryptospiridion smaller than a fleck of talcom powder which squashes and elongates and bursts in the warmth of the gut. Everything is measured twice and we have stand-bys and shut-offs. This is what keeps you and me alive, this is the real work of the river

This is the thirst that draws the soul, beginning
at these three boreholes and radial collectors.
Whatever pumps and gravitates and gathers
in town reservoirs secretly can you follow it rushing
under manholes in the straggle of the streets
being gridded and channelled up
even as he taps his screwdriver on a copper pipe
and fills a glass. That this is the thirst that streaks
his throat and chips away at his bones between lifting
the glass and contact whatever sands the tongue,
this draws his eyehole to this space among
two thirds weight water and still swallowing.
That now and then it puts him in a stare
going over the tree-lit river in his car

Jan Coo! Jan Coo!
have you any idea what goes into water?

I have verified the calibration records

have you monitored for colour and turbidity?

I'm continually sending light signals through it, my
    parameters are back to back

was it offish? did you increase the magnetite?

180 tonnes of it. I have bound the debris and skimmed
    the supernatant

have you in so doing dealt with the black inert matter?

in my own way. I have removed the finest particles

did you shut down all inlets?

I added extra chlorine

have you countervailed against decay?
have you created for us a feeling of relative
    invulnerability?

I do my best. I walk under the rapid gravity filters, under the
clarifier with the weight of all the water for the Torbay area
going over me, it's a lot for one man to carry on his shoulders.

wave the car on, let him pass, he has
sufficiently conducted himself under the pressure of
    self-repetition,
tomorrow it continues with the dripdripdripdrip of
    samples,
polyelectrolite and settlementation and twizzling scum
    and.

Exhausted almost to a sitstill,
letting the watergnats gather, for I am no longer   the river meets the
able to walk except on a slope,   Sea at the foot of
                                                          Totnes Weir

I inch into the weir's workplace,
pace volume light dayshift nightshift
water being spooled over, now

my head is about to slide – furl up my eyes,
give in to the crash of
surrendering riverflesh falling, I

come to in the sea I dream
at the foot of the weir, out here asleep
when the level fills and fills and covers the footpath,

the stones go down, the little mounds of sand
and sticks go down, the slatted walkway
sways in flood, canoes glide among trees,

trees wade, bangles of brash on branches,
it fills, it rains, the moon
spreads out floating above its sediment,

and a child secretly sleepwalks
under the frisky sound of the current
out all night, closed in an egg of water

(Sleep was at work and from the mind the mist   a dreamer
spread up like litmus to the moon, the rain
hung glittering in mid-air when I came down
and found a little patch of broken schist
under the water's trembling haste.
It was so bright, I picked myself a slate
as flat as a round pool and threw my whole
thrust into it, as if to skim my soul.
and nothing lies as straight as that stone's route
over the water's wobbling light;
it sank like a feather falls, not quite
in full possession of its weight.

I saw a sheet of seagulls suddenly
flap and lift with a loud clap and up
into the pain of flying, cry and croup
and crowd the light as if in rivalry
to peck the moon-bone empty
then fall all anyhow with arms spread out
and feet stretched forwards to the earth again.
They stood there like a flock of sleeping men
with heads tucked in, surrendering to the night.
whose forms from shoulder height
sank like a feather falls, not quite
in full possession of their weight.

There one dreamed bare clothed only in his wings
and one slept floating on his own reflection
whose outline was a point without extension.
At his wits' end to find the flickerings

27

of his few names and bones and things,
someone stood shouting inarticulate
descriptions of a shape that came and went
all night under the soft malevolent
rotating rain. and woke twice in a state
of ecstasy to hear his shout
sink like a feather falls, not quite
in full possession of its weight.

Tillworkers, thieves and housewives, all enshrined
in sleep, unable to look round; night vagrants,
prisoners on dream-bail, children without parents,
free-trading, changing, disembodied, blind
dreamers of every kind;
even corpses, creeping disconsolate
with tiny mouths, not knowing, still in tears,
still in their own small separate atmospheres,
rubbing the mould from their wet hands and feet
and lovers in mid-flight
all sank like a feather falls, not quite
in full possession of their weight.

And then I saw the river's dream-self walk
down to the ringmesh netting by the bridge
to feel the edge of shingle brush the edge
of sleep and float a world up like a cork
out of its body's liquid dark.
Like in a waterfall one small twig caught
catches a stick, a straw, a sack, a mesh
of leaves, a fragile wickerwork of floodbrash,
I saw all things catch and reticulate
into this dreaming of the Dart
that sinks like a feather falls, not quite
in full possession of its weight)

I wake wide in a swim of
seagulls, scavengers, monomaniac, mad

rubbish pickers, mating blatantly, screaming

and slouch off scumming and flashing and hatching
    flies
to the milk factory, staring at routine things:

looking down the glass lines: bottles on belts going round bends. Watching out for breakages, working nights. Building up prestige. Me with my hands under the tap, with my brain coated in a thin film of milk. In the fridge, in the warehouse, wearing ear-protectors.

I'm in a rationalised set-up, a superplant. Everything's stainless and risk can be spun off by centrifugal motion: blood, excrement, faecal matter from the farms

have you forgotten the force that orders the world's
    fields
and sets all cities in their sites, this nomad
pulling the sun and moon, placeless in all places,
born with her stones, with her circular bird-voice,
carrying everywhere her quarters?

I'm in milk, 600,000,000 gallons a week.

processing, separating, blending. Very precise quantities of raw milk added to skim, piped into silos, little screwed outlets pouring out milk to be sampled. Milk clarified milk homogenised and pasteurised and when it rains, the river comes under the ringmesh netting, full of non-potable water. All those pathogens and spoilage organisms! We have to think of our customers. We take pride in safety, we discard thirty bottles either side of a breakage. We've got weights and checks and trading standards

and a duck's nest in the leat with four blue eggs

and all the latest equipment, all stainless steel so immaculate you can see your soul in it, in a hairnet, in white overalls and safety shoes.

It's a rush, a sploosh of sewage, twenty thousand cubic metres being pumped in, stirred and settled out and wasted off, looped back, macerated, digested, clarified and returned to the river. I'm used to the idea. I fork the screenings out – a stink-mass of loopaper and whathaveyou, rags cottonbuds, you name it. I measure the intake through a flume and if there's too much, I waste it off down the stormflow, it's not my problem.

When you think of all the milk we get from Unigate, fats and proteins and detergents foaming up and the rain and all the public sewers pumping in all day, it's like a prisoner up to his neck in water in a cell with only a hand-pump to keep himself conscious, the whole place is always on the point of going under.

So we only treat the primary flow, we keep it moving up these screws, we get the solids settled out and then push the activated sludge back through. Not much I can do.

I walk on metal grilles above smelly water, I climb the ladder, I stand on a bridge above a brown lagoon, little flocs of sludge and clarified liquor spilling over the edge of the outer circle. The bridge is turning very slowly, sweeping the spill-off round and I'm thinking illicit sneaking thoughts – no one can see me up here, just me and machinery and tiny organisms.

I'm in charge as far as Dartmoor, the metabolism of the whole South West, starting with clouds and flushing down through buildings and bodies into this underground grid of pipes, all ending up with me up here on my bridge – a flare of methane burning off blue at one end of the works and a culvert of clean water discharging out the other end, twenty BOD, nine ammonia, all the time, as and when

It happened when oak trees were men
when water was still water.
There was a man, Trojan born,
a footpad, a fighter:

Brutus, grandson of Aeneas.
But he killed his parents.
He shut his heart and sailed away
with a gang of exiled Trojans;

a hundred down and outs the sea
uninterestedly threw
from one hand to the other, where
to wash this numbness to?

An island of undisturbed woods,
rises in the waves,
a great spire of birdsong
out of a nave of leaves.

There a goddess calls them,
'Take aim, take heart,
Trojans, you've got to sail
till the sea meets the Dart.

Where salmon swim with many a glittering
and herons flare and fold,
look for a race of freshwater
filling the sea with gold.

If you can dip your hand down
and take a fish first go
or lean out and pick an oyster
while a seal stares at you,

then steer your ships into its pull
when the tide's on the rise
at full moon when the river
grazes the skirts of the trees

and row as far as Totnes
and there get out and stand,
outcasts of the earth, kings
of the green island England.'

Thirty days homeless on the sea,
twelve paces, then turn,
shacked in a lean-to ship,
windlash and sunburn.

Thirty days through a blue ring
suspended above nothing,
themselves and their flesh-troubled souls
in sleep, twisting and soothing.

They wake among landshapes,
the jut-ends of continents
foreign men with throats to slit;
a stray rock full of cormorants.

They sail into the grey-eyed rain,
a race of freshwater
fills the sea with flecks of peat,
sparrows shoal and scatter.

And when they dip their hands down
they can touch the salmon,
oysters on either side,
shelduck and heron.

So they steer into its pull
when the tide's on the rise,
at full moon when the river
grazes the skirts of the trees.

Silent round Dittisham bend,
each pause of the oar
they can hear the tiny sounds
of river crabs on the shore.

A fox at Stoke Gabriel,
a seal at Duncannon,
they sing round Sharpham bend
among the jumping salmon.

At Totnes, limping and swaying,
they set foot on the land.
There's a giant walking towards them,
a flat stone in each hand:

stonewaller

You get upriver stones and downriver stones. Beyond Totnes bridge and above Longmarsh the stones are horrible grey chunks, a waste of haulage, but in the estuary they're slatey flat stones, much darker, maybe it's to do with the river's changes. Every beach has its own species, I can read them, volcanic, sedimentary, red sandstone, they all nest in the Dart, but it's the rock that settles in layers and then flakes and cracks that gives me my flat walling stone.

The estuary's my merchant. I go pretty much the length and breadth of it scrudging stuff for some tiny stretch of wall, looking for the fault lines and the scabs of crystals and the natural coigns which are right-angled stones for corners.

I'm struggling now to find the really lovely stones I dream of: maroon stones, perfect ellipses – but it's not just stones, sometimes huge bits of wood with the texture of water still in them in the plane of movement, a kind of camber.

I've made barns, sheds, chicken houses, goose huts, whatever I require, just putting two and two together, having a boat and a bit of space that needs squaring; which is how everything goes with me, because you see I'm a gatherer, an amateur, a scavenger, a comber, my whole style's a stone wall, just wedging together what happens to be lying about at the time.

I love this concept of drift, meaning driven, deposited by a current of air or water. Like how I came by the boat, someone just phoned and said I've got this eighteen-foot crabber and one thing led to another. Here I am now with a clinker-built launch.

But it's off the river at the moment, it gets a lot of wear and tear going aground on hard rocks and carrying a tonnage of stone around. I haven't worked it for six months, hence my agitated state, I keep looking over my shoulder, I dream my skin's flaking off and silting up the house; because the boat's my aerial, my instrument, connects me into the texture of things, as I keep saying, the grain, the drift of water which I couldn't otherwise get a hold on.

A tree-line, a slip-lane, a sight-line, an eye-hole, whatever it is, when you're chugging past Sharpham on a fine evening, completely flat, the water just glows. You get this light different from anything on land, as if you're keeping a different space, you're in a more wobbly element like a wheelbarrow, you can feel the whole earth tipping, the hills shifting up and down, shedding stones as if everything's a kind of water

Oceanides Atlanta Proserpina Minerva   boat voices

yachts with their river-shaking engines

Lizzie of Lymington Doris of Dit'sum

bending the firey strands under their keels, sheathed in the flying fields and fleeing the burden of being

two sailing boats, like prayers towing their wooden
    tongues
Naini Tal, Nereid of Quarr

and the sailmaker grabbing his sandwich,
the rich man bouncing his powerboat like a gym shoe,

the boatyard manager, thriving in the narrow margin between storing boats and keeping them moving, costing and delegating, structuring deals and wrapping up proposals

the shipwright, the caulker, the countersunk copper
    nail

there goes the afternoon, faster than the rowers
    breathe, they lever and spring
and a skiff flies through like a needle worked loose from
    its compass

under the arch where Mick luvs Trudi
and Jud's heart
has the arrow locked through it

six corn-blue dinghies banging together
Liberty Belle, Easily Led, Valentine, L'Amour, White
    Rose and Fanny

and there goes Westerly Corsair Golden Cloud and
    Moonfire
Windweaver Sunshadow Seawolf

in the shine of a coming storm when the kiosk is
    closed
and gulls line up and gawp on the little low wall

there goes a line of leaves, there goes winter there goes the river
at the speed of the woods coming into flower a little slower than
the heron a little slower than a make-do boat running to heel
with only a few galvanised bits and a baler between you and your
watery soul

there goes spring, there goes the lad from Kevicks
sailing to New Zealand in a tiny catamaran to find his
    girlfriend,
a wave washes out his stove, he's eating pasta soaked in
    seawater
and by the time he gets there she's with someone else

Troll, Fluff, Rank, Bruckless,
Bootle Bumtrink, Fisher 25,
Tester, Pewter, Whistler, Smiler
Jezail, Saith Seren, Pianola, Windfola,
Nanuk, Callooh, Shereefah

it's taken twenty years,   boatbuilder
every bit of spare cash,
it started as a dream, I did some sketches,
I had to build myself a shed to make it in

Freeby
Moody
Loopy Lou

every roll of fibre glass two hundred quid, it has to be
sandwiched round foam and resined, the whole thing rubbed
over with powdered glass and sanded by hand, but you can make
fantastic shapes: eighteen drawers in the galley not one the same
size, two rudders – you could sell them to the Tate

Checkmate Knot Shore

now if this was a wooden boat you'd have to steam the planks,
they used to peg them on the tide line to get salt into the timber;
you can still see grown oak boats, where you cut the bilge beams
straight out of the trees, keeping the line sweet, fairing it by eye,
it's a different mindset – when I was a boy all boats leaked like a
basket, if you were sailing you were bailing

Merry Fiddler Music Maker Island Life Fiesta

but give us a couple more years we'll be out of here, in the Med,
soaking up the sun, lying on the netting watching dolphins,
swapping a boatnail for a fish, we'll be away from all these cars,
all this rain, that's what the dream is that's what this boat is – for
twenty years now our only way out's been building it

like a ship the shape of flight
or like the weight that keeps it upright
or like a skyline crossed by breath
or like the planking bent beneath
or like a glint or like a gust
or like the lofting of a mast

such am I who flits and flows
and seeks and serves and swiftly goes –
the ship sets sail, the weight is thrown,
the skyline shifts, the planks groan,

the glint glides, the gust shivers
the mast sways and so does water

then like a wave the flesh of wind
or like the flow-veins on the sand
or like the inkling of a fish
or like the phases of a splash
or like an eye or like a bone
or like a sandflea on a stone

such am I who flits and flows
and seeks and serves and swiftly goes –
the wave slides in, the sand lifts,
the fish fades, the splash drifts,
the eye blinks, the bone shatters,
the sandflea jumps and so does water

Back in the days when I was handsome and the river   salmon netsman and
was just river –   poacher

not all these buoys everywhere that trip your net so that you've
got to cut the headrope and the mesh goes fshoo like a zip.
Terrifying.
And there was so many salmon you could sit up to your knees in
dead fish keeping your legs warm.
I used to hear the tramp tramp tramp under my window of men
going down to the boats at three in the morning.

Low water, dead calm.

You don't know what goes on down there.
You go to bed, you switch out the light.
There's three of us in the pub with our hands shaking:
Have a beer mate, you're going out ...
We daren't say anything, they can guess what we're onto
because the adrenalin's up and we're
jumping about like sea trout eeeeeeeeeee
I haven't calmed down since a week ago,
I was standing under a sheer wall

with a bailiff above me flashing his torch over the river.
I put my hand up and touched his boot
and it's making my hair fall out remembering it.
Drink up now. Last orders. Low water. Dead calm.

When the sun goes down the wind drops.
It's so quiet you could fall asleep at the paddles.
That's when you can hear them jumping –
slap slap – you've got to be onto it.
I had a dog once who could sense a salmon.

That's your legal fisherman, he's watching and
    listening,
he's got a seine net and he hauls out from the shore
    and
back in a curve, like this.
But more than likely he's got a legal right hand and a
rogue left hand and when he's out left-handed,
he just rows a mesh net straight across the river – a
    bloody wall.
In twenty minutes he's covered the cost of the net,
in an hour he's got a celebration coming.
That's where the crack is, that's when fishing pays.

Or if it's dawn or nightfall, the river's the weird colour
    of the sky,
you can see a voler as much as two miles away.
That's the unique clean line a salmon makes in water
and you make a speckle for which way he's heading.

Your ears are twitching for the bailiff,
the car engine, the rustle in the bushes.
Bam! Lights come on, you ditch the net –
stop running, x, we know who you are.

There's a scuffle. The skill's to time it right, to row out
    fast and shoot your net fast over the stern,

a risky operation when you're leaning out and the boat
    wobbles –
I saw a man fallover the edge once:
oo oo oooo ...

Our boat went under between the wharf and steamer
    quay.
We'd got weights on board, more than you're meant to
and we were all three of us in the water. One drowned.
It's a long story, you've got to judge the tide

You've got to judge the tide precisely, you draw a
    semicircle back to land.
One man's up there pulling the net in, knuckles to
    ground, so the catch doesn't spill out under,
which is hard work till it gets to the little eddy offshore
    and then the river gathers it in for you.
You can see them in the bunt of the net torpedoing
    round.
Sometimes a salmon'll smack your arm a significant
    knock, so you pull it right up the mud.
Some people would perceive it dangerous, but we know
    what we're doing,
even when it's mud up to our thighs, we know the places
    where the dredger's taken the sand away
Foul black stuff, if you got out there you might well
    disappear
and people do die in this river.

Three men on an oystering expedition,
the tide flowing in, the wind coming down,
on a wide bit of the river.
They filled the boat too full, they all drowned.

Where are you going? Flat Owers.   oyster gatherers
Who's Owers? Ours.
A paddock of sand mid-river
two hours either side of low water.

Can I come over?
All kinds of weather
when the wind spins you round
in your fish-tin boat with its four-stroke engine.

Who lives here?
Who dies here?
Only oysters and often
the quartertone quavers of an oyster-catcher.

Keep awake, keep listening.
The tide comes in fast
and after a while it
looks like you're standing on the water

still turning and shaking your oyster bags.
Already the sea taste
wets and sways the world – what now?
Now back to the river.

Feel this rain.
The only light's
the lichen tinselling the trees.
And when it's gone, Flat Owers

is ours. We mouth our joy.
Oysters, out of sight of sound.
A million rippled
life-masks of the river.

I thought it was a corpse once when I had a seal in the
   net – huge – a sea lion.
They go right up to the weir.
They hang around by the catch waiting for a chance.

That's nothing – I almost caught a boat once.
On an S-bend. Not a sound.
Pitch dark, waiting for the net to fill, then
BOOM BOOM BOOM – a pleasure boat

with full disco comes flashing round the corner.
What you call a panic bullet –
ten seconds to get the net in,
two poachers pulling like mad
in slow motion strobe lights
and one man, pissed, leans over the side and says
hellooooooooooooooo?

But if you're lucky, at the last knockings it's a salmon with his
great hard bony nose –
you hit him with a napper and he goes on twitching in the boat
asking for more, more to come, more salmon to come.
But there aren't many more these days. They get caught off
Greenland in the monofilaments.
That's why we're cut-throats on weekdays.

We have been known to get a bit fisticuffs –
boats have been sunk, nets set fire.
Once I waited half an hour and
hey what's happening, some tosser's poaching the stretch
    below me,
so I leg it downriver and make a bailiff noise in the bushes

And if you find a poacher's net, you just get out your pocket
knife and shred it like you were ripping his guts.

whose side are you on?
I've grown up on this river,
I look after this river,
what's your business?

beating the other boats to the best places:
sandy pools up Sharpham where the salmon holds back
    to rub the sea-lice off his belly.
He'll hold back waiting for the pressure of water
or maybe it's been raining and washed oil off the roads
    or nitrates and God knows what else
and he doesn't like his impressions up the weir.

Some days the river's dark black – that's the moor water.
But the dredger's got rid of those pools now. We tie up
    at Duncannon now.

We go there after work, we dash down a cup of tea and a
sandwich, then lie about chatting on the stones

and we're down the Checkers every Friday evening,
saying nothing, playing yooker,
in the bogs in twos and threes, sorting out the order of
    the River –
You're Mondays, you're everything down from Am,
my place is the blind spot under the bridge
and if anyone else turns up, break their legs

why is this jostling procession of waters,
its many strands overclambering one another,
so many word-marks, momentary traces
in wind-script of the world's voices,
why is it so bragging and surrendering,
love-making, spending, working and wandering,
so stooping to look, so unstopping,
so scraping and sharpening and smoothing and
    wrapping,
why is it so sedulously clattering
so like a man mechanically muttering
so sighing, so endlessly seeking
to hinge his fantasies to his speaking,
all these scrambled and screw-like currents
and knotty altercations of torrents,
why is this interweaving form as contiguously gliding
as two sisters, so entwined, so dividing,
so caught in this dialogue that keeps
washing into the cracks of their lips
and spinning in the small hollows
of their ears and egos
this huge vascular structure

why is this flickering water
with its blinks and side-long looks
with its language of oaks
and clicking of its slatey brooks
why is this river not ever
able to leave until it's over?

Dartmouth and Kingsweir –   ferryman
two worlds, like two foxes in a wood,
and each one can hear the wind-fractured
closeness of the other.

I work the car ferry, nudge it over with a pilot boat,
backwards and forwards for twenty three years.

Always on the way over – to or fro –
and feeling inward for a certain sliding feeling
that loosens the solidity of the earth,
he makes himself a membrane through which everyone
    passes into elsewhere
like a breath flutters its ghost across glass.

I was working it the night the Penhilly lifeboat went
    down:
soaking, terrified, frozen – the last man out on the river.
But I never saw any ghosts. I came home drowning.
I walked into the house and there was my beautiful
    red-haired wife,
there wasn't a man over twenty-five that didn't fancy
    her.

I think of her in autumn, when the trees go this
    amazing colour round Old Mill Creek.
I go down there and switch off my engine.   Silence.
After a while you hear the little sounds of the ebb.
Or in winter, you can hear stalks of ice splintering under
    the boat.

Wholly taken up with the detail to hand,
he tunes his tiller, he rubs the winter between his fingers.

On a good day, I can hear the wagtails over the engine.
Or I'll hear this cough like a gentleman in the water,
I turn round and it's a seal.

Swift fragmentary happenings

that ferry him between where things are now
and why, disengaging his eyes from the question

naval cadet

twenty years old and I already know knots and lowering boats. I
know radar and sonar, I can cross the gym without touching the
floor. I can nearly handle a two-engine picket boat, turn it on a
sixpence and bring it alongside.

I'm officer-quality, I've been brutalised into courage. You could
fire me from a frigate and I'd be a high-kill sea-skimming
weapon, I'd hit the target standing to attention.

I've got serious equipment in my head: derricks and davits, sea-
pistols, fins and wings and noise signatures. When the Threat
comes I'll be up an hour before it with my boots bulled and my
bed pulled up. Then down the path to Sandquay and encounter
it whatever it is. I've got the gear and the capability.

Every morning I bang my head against the wall, I let it shatter
and slowly fill up with water. I'm prepared you see. I jog round
the block, I go like hell and there's the sea the whole of it
measuring itself against my body, how strong am I? I can really
run, I take steps two at a time, I salute the painted Britannia.

I've got the knack of fear, I've done two acquaints in a dinghy,
just enough to get the feel of the wind, a hostile at the end of a
rope. Would I float? If the hull was damaged, how long can I
hold my breath?

the day the ship went down and five
policemen made a circle round

the sand and something half imagined
was born in blankets up the beach

all that day a dog was running
backwards forwards, shaking the water's
feathers from its fur and down
the sea-front noone came for chips

and then the sun went out and almost
madly the Salvation Army's
two strong women raised and tapped
their softest tambourines and someone

stared at the sea between his shoes
and I who had the next door grave
undressed without a word and lay
in darkness thinking of the sea

I remember when I was a boy   rememberer
born not more than a mile from where I am now

a whole millennium going by in the form of a wave

Dad was pilot on the Dart
at two in the morning in a force nine gale
flashing a torch to lead her in
you can see the current sliding through that moment

over a thousand tons of ship plus cargo
the quay getting closer at full speed and at a certain pace

you get this pause superimposed on water I remember

two sisters, Mrs Allen and Mrs Fletcher
used to row the plums across from Dittisham
and one dawn there were seven crusader ships
in the same steady stream of wind

it isn't easy to make out
in driving rain through water when you consider
your eyes are made mostly of movement

the cod fleet and the coal hulks and the bunkers from the
    Tyne and
a man sitting straight-up, reading a book in the bows
    while his ship was sinking   (Humphrey Gilbert)

but that was way back, when a chap made his living
    from his wits,
when I still had my parting in the middle and you could
    pull up
forty thousand pilchards in one draft

I stood here, I saw a whole flock of water migrating,
I saw two square-rigged barges carrying
deals, battens, scantling, lathwood
going out again with empty casks,
bags of trickling particles, bones, salts

Lew Bird, Stormy Croker,   former pilots on the
tiny spasms of time cross-fixed into water   Dart

and that same night, Dad took a merchant ship out
and left her at Castle ledge and she was bombed
and I saw the flames for hours up over that hill there

    crabbers

two brothers, both sea-fishers. Left school at fifteen and joined
the supercrabbers, big boats working out of Dartmouth and
when I say working

Say it's stormy, you walk a thousand miles just to stand upright.
Each crab pot seventy pounds and the end ones that weigh the
net down about the weight of a washing machine, that's twenty
tonnes of gear per day and only five hours sleep. Plus it's high
risk. We were out in a hurricaine twenty miles off the Sillies.

No greenery – when you're at sea it's all sea. Then you head for
Dartmouth and fifteen miles away you can smell the land, you
smell silage, you see lights and fires. You've got a thousand
pounds for a week's work, you've got five days to enjoy yourself.
I went mad, I sent my wife champagne in a taxi.

I taxi'd to Plymouth, gave the cabbie lunch and paid him to wait all day for me.

We got a reputation, smashing up the town a bit, what could we do? Age fifteen we were big money, it was like crabs were a free commodity, we could go on pulling them from the sea year after year, it was like a trap for cash. Not to mention what some crabbers pull up, they don't always set their pots where the crabs are.

Ten years of that you pay for it with your body. Arthritis in the thumbs, elbows, knees, shoulders, back. A friend of ours died twice lifting pots, literally died, he had two heart attacks and got up again.

So now we're rod-and-lining off small piss-pot boats and setting nets for whatever. Some days we don't catch anything. Don't catch don't eat. Me and my dog went six days without food last winter.

But we're fisherman, Matt, we won't starve

                                Sid, we're allergic
                                      to fish

But tell me another job where you can see the whole sunrise every morning. No clocking in, no time bell. In summer you can dive in, see whales jumping, catch turtles the size of a dory. You slap your hands on the boatside and tell me another job where a dolphin spooks you, looks you straight in the eye and lets you touch him. You don't know what you are till you've seen that

they start the boat, they climb
as if over the river's vertebrae
out of its body into the wings of the sea
rounding the Mew Stone, the last bone of the Dart
where the shag stands criticising the weather
and rolls of seals haul out and scrabble away
and the seal-watcher on his wave-ski
shouts and waves and slowly paddles out of sight.

47

I steer my wave-ski into caves
horrible to enter alone
The fur, the hair, the fingernails, the bones.

Flick out the torch, the only thread between down
    here and daylight
and count five while the sea suckles and settles.
Self-maker, speaking its meaning over mine.

At low water
I swim up a dog-leg bend into the cliff,
the tide slooshes me almost to the roof

and float inwards into the trembling sphere
of one freshwater drip drip drip
where my name disappears and the sea slides in to
    replace it.

There the musky fishy genital smell
of things not yet actual: shivering impulses, shadows,
    propensities,
little amorous movements, quicksilver strainings and
    restrainings:

each winter they gather here,
twenty seals in this room behind the sea, all swaddled
and tucked in fat, like the soul in is cylinder of flesh.

With their grandmother mouths, with their dog-soft
    eyes, asking
who's this moving in the dark? Me.
This is me, anonymous, water's soliloquy,

all names, all voices, Slip-Shape, this is Proteus,
whoever that is, the shepherd of the seals,
driving my many selves from cave to cave ...